# HOW I GOT MY SEX DRIVE BACK

TARUN GILL

Invincible Publishers

First published in India in 2019

©2019 Invincible Publishers, All Rights Reserved

ISBN : 978-938-8333-64-1

Invincible Publishers

Registered Address: 201A, SAS Tower, Sector 38, Gurgaon-122003

Printed at Thomson Press (India) LTD

No part of this publication may be reproduced or stored in a retrieval system, or transmitted in any form or by any means, electronic, mechanical, photocopying, recording or otherwise, without the prior permission of the publishers.

This book and the program is not intended as a substitute for the medical advice of physicians. The reader should regularly consult a physician in matters relating to his/her health and particularly with respect to any symptoms that may require diagnosis or medical attention. (health, alternative healing)

Like any sport involving speed, equipment, balance and environmental factors, training for six pack abs poses some inherent risk. The authors and publisher advise readers to take full responsibility for their safety and know their limits.Also note, every body type is different

*Dedicated to my father*
*Joginder Gill*

# Acknowledgement

Want to thank so many people who made this book happen.

My mother, who has been my support system

My wife, who lived with my chest fat

My mentor, Aditya Ghosh, who believed in me, when noone else did.

My mentor and friend, Nick Parmar, who stood by me

My Friend, Amit Yadav, who got me in the fitness industry

Each one has a role to play and I would not have been here without them.

SATNAM VAHEGURU

# Introduction

I find it extremely funny that in a country like India with a second largest population, no one really talks about sex openly. But the facts states that people in India love sex to produce children. And God forbids, if you have a sex problem, you literally had it.

I hate to admit, besides many other problems in life, i also developed a sex problem in my early thirties. Unlike most of the people, i will not hide it but will try to keep it as transparent as i can. Because this problem at some point in your life, every man would face. The problem of Erectile dysfunction.

**What is erectile dysfunction**

It is the man's inability to either get or keep the erection firm for a sustained period of time necessary for sex. In simple terms, you have a problem with erection and you can't indulge in any sexual intercourse with your partner. I mean you can, but you won't get any hardness.

Its like you would be wearing a superman dress, but would have no super powers. Can you imagine a problem like that. Who on God's earth was the first one identified with this problem.

Lets admit it. We are men, we all love sex. We can make anything sound so sexual, because we are thinking about sex 24 7. How is that even remotely possible that something you are so obsessed about refuses to perform or function. This is a complete anti climax.

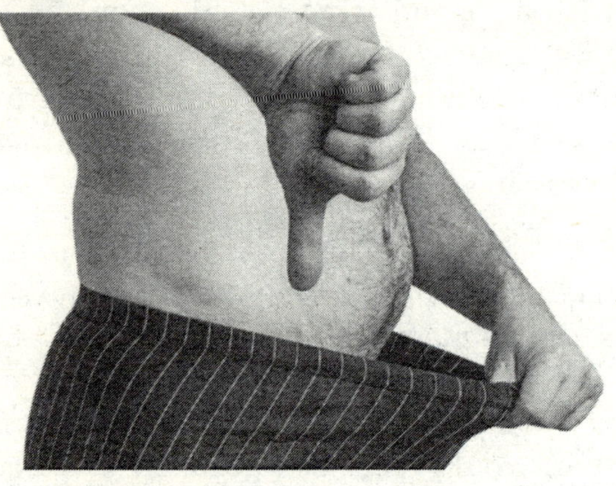

**Here is another situation.**

You go to a party and find a woman of your dreams. Things get out of control and you find yourself alone with her in the room. As you indulge in foreplay, you realise that there is no hardness or what most people would call it "no wood". But the woman of your dreams is all excited and waiting of you to make the next obvious move. And this is where erectile dysfunction kicks in. You can't get it up.

What would you do in a situation like that? I wish i had a satisfactory answer for all of you, but unfortunately i don't. I can only share how i got out of this hole (pun unintended). The above situation happened with me and when i realized that my junior is not responding, i obviously got frustrated, but didn't let it show on my face.

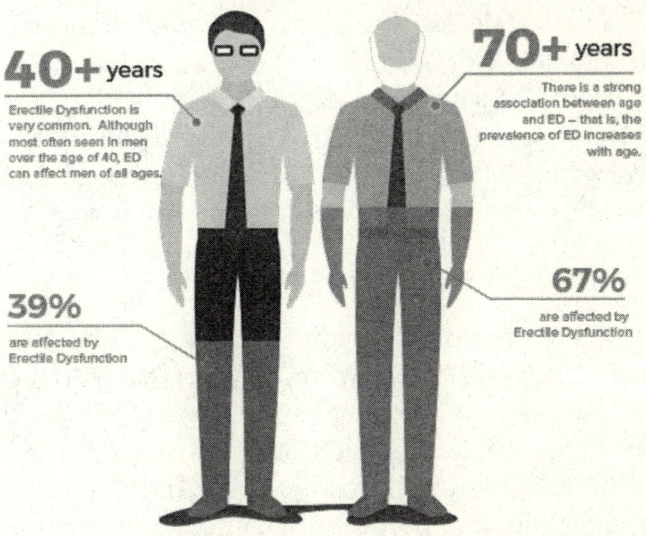


I took out my phone as if it got vibrated indicating there is a new message. And then emotionally reacted to it. Damn! I have to make an urgent phone call. And that phone call was only to bail me out of this situation. " I have to leave, something has come up. Let me drop you home" were my words to her.

No matter how good an actor you are, a girl will never believe you. Because as i said, men only thinks about sex and girls know that. So a man refusing to have sex with a woman, only implies that there is something wrong with this man. And that problem got to be sexual. Its no rocket science, its erectile dysfunction baby.

It plays with your mind

Yes it is common

You would be surprised to know that this problem has not become very common especially in India. Do you know there are more than 10 million cases reported of Erectile dysfunction every year in India. This is a huge number in the world's second largest populated country.

**Causes**

There could be many causes for erectile dysfunction but what in most cases, the causes are generally psychological in nature. One of the biggest reason which affected sex drive of millions of men in India, is stress. And more the stress levels, the harder it becomes for a man to perform sexually.

But there could be many other medical reasons as well which includes but not limited to high blood pressure, diabetes etc.

But the core of every sexual problem lies in your mind. Once it hits your mind, that you can't perform, it will take you a really long time to come out of it. So it is as simple, don't let it affect your mind. I realised this after months of going through the torture of non performance.

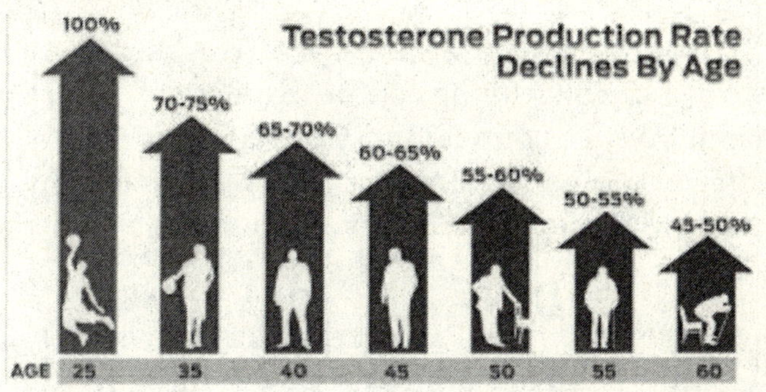


## Stress

I didn't really know what stress actually was until i faced this demon of low sex drive. I had only heard of such things. But once it happened with me, i actually experienced the horror of it.

We don't realise the amount of stress levels, our body usually takes on a daily basis. And that stress could be related to job, profession or even your own personal growth. That stress not only ruin our health but also have a negative affect on your sex drive.

## How it began

In the beginning of my thirties, i was one of the victims. A time come in your life when you begin to seek answers of where your life is going.

It may have hit some people and some may yet to experience it. But the early thirties was the point of life where i had to transition myself onto something which made me happy.

I was a corporate employee, working forty hours a week, living on a handsome salary cheque. With a sound education background, my career was on a right track and i was eyeing my next promotion to be the vice president of my company.

But deep down, i was never happy with my life. Then i started evaluating everything in my life. What was going wrong!

I was married to a beautiful girl who has always been my pillar of strength. My parents loved me for what i had done in my life. Then what was missing?

This thinking never stopped. It only got worse with years. So much so, that i started losing interest in my job. This suddenly started affecting my job performance which invariably had an affect on my sexual health.

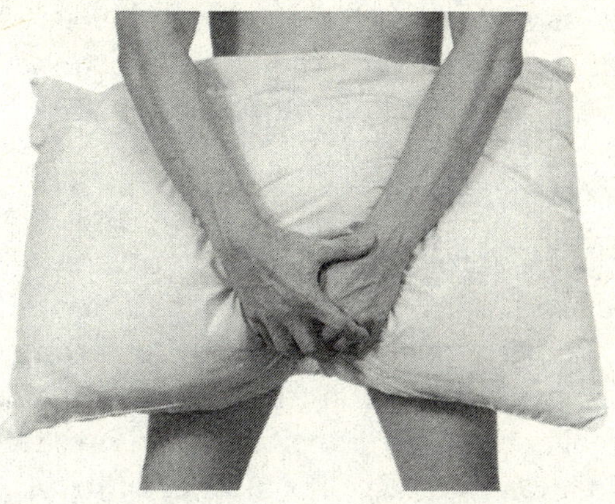

## Things got worse

Because i was frustrated, i took out all my angst on my work out and training. I was also living with body image issues of having male boobs. Have written a separate book on my struggle of losing male boobs called " How i fixed my chest fat".

To improve my body image, i started experimenting with anabolic steroids. My only goal was to minimise my chest fat which may give me more self confidence. Even though with my effort and training, i was able to minimise my chest fat but things went south with my sexual health.

For the first time i experienced no morning hardness. I thought may be it is one of those days! But it became a pattern. I even lost the desire the have any sex.

This made me consult many doctors and all said one thing. Stress and steroid usage have lowered my body's testosterone levels. This is when i researched the term testosterone extensively, which made me write this book

## What is testosterone

Test is predominantly a male hormone, which is associated with sex drive and libido. Even though women ovaries make testosterone but that is in very limited quantity. The production of test in males typically starts when they are twelve years old and gradually dips after age thirty.

Test levels take a hit and drop every year after a man turns thirty. A normal dip in the levels is understandable but a considerable drop is alarming!

Testosterone affects on the body

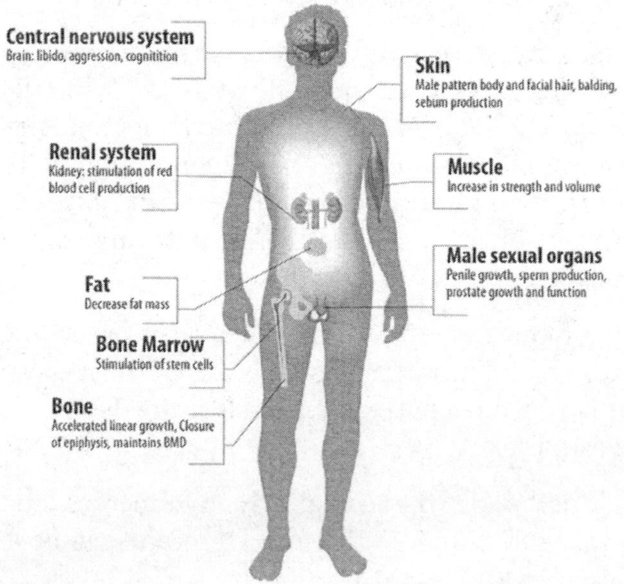

**Central nervous system**
Brain: libido, aggression, cognitition

**Skin**
Male pattern body and facial hair, balding, sebum production

**Renal system**
Kidney: stimulation of red blood cell production

**Muscle**
Increase in strength and volume

**Male sexual organs**
Penile growth, sperm production, prostate growth and function

**Fat**
Decrease fat mass

**Bone Marrow**
Stimulation of stem cells

**Bone**
Accelerated linear growth, Closure of epiphysis, maintains BMD

## Testing your test levels

How do you know if your test levels are low? Even though low libido itself is quite a sign of low test levels, but it is always recommended to get the medical test done for your testosterone.

A blood test can easily gauge and determine your existing test levels. There is lot of test floating in your bloodstream, which will tell you the current levels. Which is exactly what i did. I got my tests done, and was shocked to see the report.

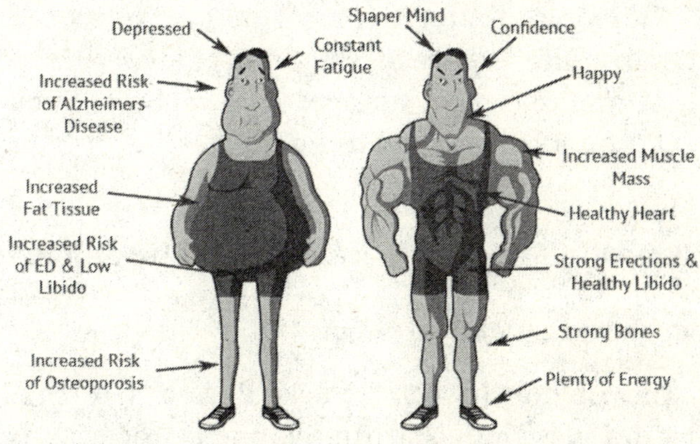


## What is the normal test range

The normal range of testosterone for most healthy male adults is between 250 and 1100 ng/dL. But what i got in my report was 26 ng/dl. What doctors told me i had a complete shut down. Which means i lost the ability to have sex.

Can you imagine a state when you are told you won't be able to have sex with such levels. It is like taking your balls by the hand and crushing them. Exactly how i felt. We have all had medical problems in the past, but a problem with manhood can crush a male ego.

## When a male ego hurts

The report not only saddened me but gave me suicidal thoughts. Imagine a life of a man who can't have sex. And the problem is such issues can't be addressed in the open, sad but true.

The worse was yet to come! How am i supposed to tell my wife. What will she think of me. Will she accept me. She may just ask for a divorce. Such crazy thoughts ruled my mind.

But i had to confront her, which i did. I remember having a tough time mustering up the courage to find the right words to tell her that i have had a sexual shutdown.

She obviously was shocked! And her first question was, how did this happen. And this is where i had to tell her everything what i have been through. Believe me, this is a very tough conversation. I shared all my past experiences with her which she was totally unaware of! And for some reason i was feeling very relieved that i had someone to talk to about such things.

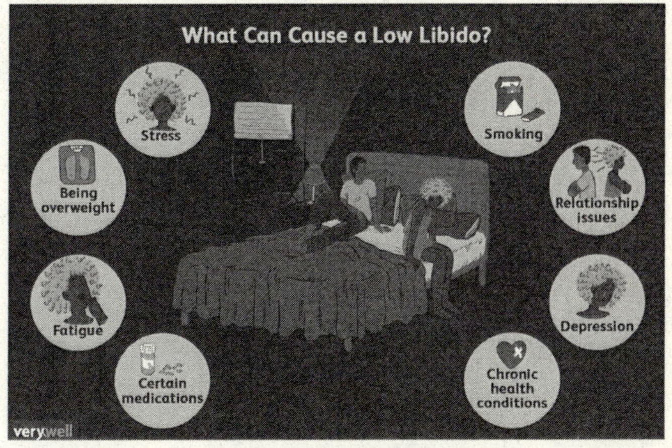


And to have a life partner like that, who would understand this situation, is a blessing. I have seen many relationships not working out due to sexual incompatibility. And this happens because the partners don't share the problems with each other. In simple words, lack of communication

## What saved my marriage

The honesty to confront my spouse, on having sexual issues saved my marriage. I see so many men having a difficult time to talk about such issues which leads to a void, ending up in a break up. My learning is to talk it out.

Here is a secret : While i was going through my low sex drive phase, i spoke to many so called expert friends on this issue. And all were experts in telling me things which i had never even heard of!

And listening to friends is the worse thing you can ever do.

One of my friends told me to try the famous blue pill, viagra. Now before you judge me, you know my reasons to try it. For people who don't know what viagra is, it is the controversial solution for erectile dysfunction.

**Is viagra safe**

Well i can only share my experience with it. On my friend's advise, i tried viagra. A guy who tried anabolic steroids to find a cure for his male boobs, is now trying viagra to fix his problem of low libido arising out of steroids. What an irony.

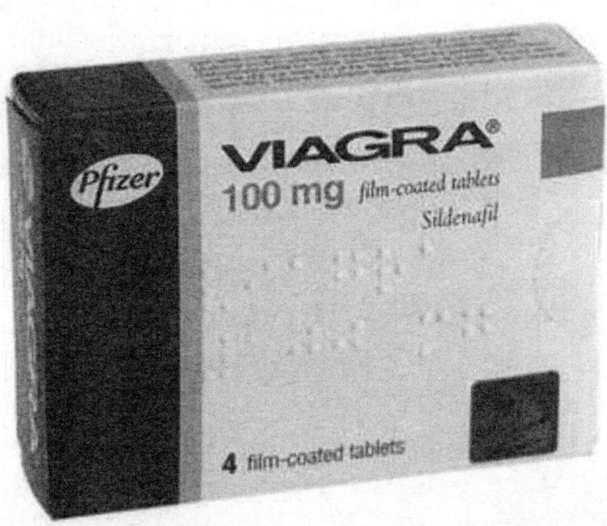

Here is my candid experience of it.

Because i had read about the side effects of viagra, i tried the 25 mg dose, which i thought was minimal. After ingesting such a pill, you would expect the pill to work in seconds, but i was not feeling anything. I was waiting for it to kick in.

Viagra typically works by relaxing the muscles. And i was only getting restless. This is where the first learning came. viagra will not work on its own, you need to be relaxed and be in the mood to have sex. I thought, it was a drug you would pop and would start working in minutes if not seconds.

Because i was thinking about my sex problem too much, i was not getting aroused. And it made me question the drug and its potency. The first question that came into my mind–Does this drug really work? Why is it not working on me, when 99% of the men in the world find it to be super effective.

And as i was thinking about drug not working, i started researching about it on the web. And i came across some literature, which highlighted to have some sexual fantasies for viagra to work. It was more than thirty minutes that i had taken this pill and it was not working.

I gave up on this drug and just lied down on bed. And suddenly the thought of my first sexual experience crossed my mind. And what i notice is that in minutes, i had a hard erection. And so much so that i could not control it. I had no other option but to masterbate.

And this is the tricky part. Even after ejaculation, the erection stayed as it is. My body was getting heated up. There was so much of sex in me which got triggered by this pill, which lead to a severe headache.

I didn't know what to do but to again masterbate. but that also didn't help. After few minutes, my vision was getting blurry. For a minute, i thought i was dying but it was just the side effect of the pill, which my body could not handle too well.

I immediately went online and checked about the side effects. And there it was. The sides which i was facing were common. And literally the effect of drug wore off almost 4- 5 hours. But thinking about these few hours, still gives me goosebumps.

Looking back, do i want to try viagra, may be not! It was too hardcore for me, but i have seen many people taking it with minimal side effects. But what i realised that this is not the solution which i want. The pill would only give me a temporary boost, what i needed was my body to make enough testosterone, for my own well being.

You don't need Testosterone for just sex but for your overall good health as well. And i knew i needed a permanent solution around it.

Don't be a Doctor

Problem with all of us is that we become doctors ourselves, start experimenting with our body. Clearly i needed to visit a doctor but i chose to self administer this problem of low testosterone which lead to even bigger problems.

Going to a sexologist in India means that you are impotent and not capable of having sex EVER. This is a mindset, which certainly needs to change. Even i thought so, that why would ever someone need a help of a sexologist. But now it has become a reality.

The stress levels and the lifestyle has had a major effect on our sex life. I even see young twenty year olds having issues with their libido. The food we are eating, the over the counter bodybuilding drugs which the youngsters are abusing to look perfect is what killing our testosterone levels.

It is ironic that the hormones men take to pack on muscle, viz testosterone is what they get deprived of when they stop injecting it after a brief period.

**The harsh reality**

You would be surprised, that most the bodybuilders across the globe have had issues with their libido in some point of their lives. It is the lifestyle that they follow. For those who don't know, let me give you a brief glimpse.

We all think that having a great body is a ticket to a woman's heart. No doubt that women like men with a great body. But imagine the same women who fell for that man with a great body having issues with performance and his sex life.

Bodybuilders or some of the fitness models with great physiques are the weakest when they start preparing for their contests. Their sex drive is the lowest when the get extremely close to their competitions.

Because most of these international bodybuilders are professional athletes, they know how to manage their sex drive and bring it back to normal. Also because they are medically monitored and do regular medical check ups.

But what about Indians, who as i mentioned earlier, have problems even visiting a doctor, let alone a sexologist.

Everyone is a self proclaimed doctor here, prescribing pills and medicines to people. It is more common in the Indian fitness industry.

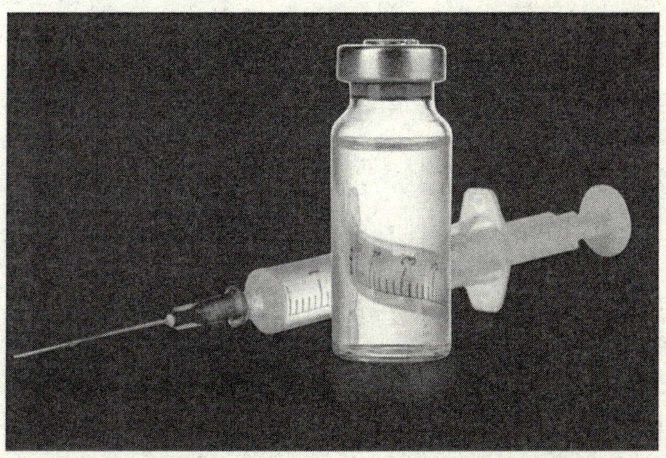

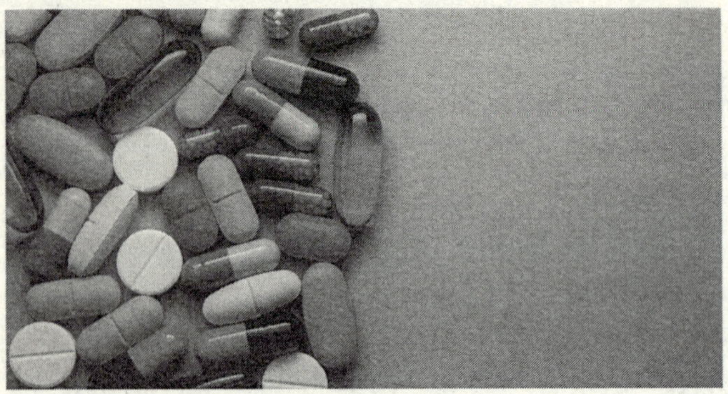

**The Guruji culture**

It is shocking to see so many youngsters being misguided by desi Gurujis who are not only prescribing pills but also injecting steroids into their bodies. Unfortunately, the fitness industry is India is still at its infancy and is at the mercy of such quacks. I am not saying all the Gurujis are like that but most of them are.

Why am i talking about Gurujis! It is these Gurujis, who are exploiting and playing with our bodies, ultimately resulting in many sexual complications.

I was one of the victims of such Guruji experiment. All i wanted was to minimise my male boobs, which had ruined my self image. And one day while i was training in the gym, i came across this trainer who saw my body and recommend i should consult his Guruji. Obviously i was desperate and could do anything to get rid of my male boobs.

On meeting him, he tried to sell me his pills and medicines claiming they will work wonders. These pills which i found out later, were made locally to increase man's testosterone levels. These pills are not only dangerous but also don't have any labels. Which means you are consuming something which you don't even know the name.

Trust me there are millions in India, who are following the same pattern. Taking pills and medicines which has no name or expiry. It is the desperation which makes us try all such measures. In my case, desperation to find solution to my problem of chest fat or male boobs.

And guess what, i bought those pills. Not only these pills were expensive but also extremely dangerous. First initial days, i felt the rush in energy, i was very active and my sex drive was insane. But after few days, the opposite happened.

I had a crash! My chest fat did not minimise on the contrary, they started looking even more prominent. Which was due to the pill, which made me active in the gym. I was losing weight from my waist line which made my chest even more protruding.

I went to that same Guruji sharing this problem. The problem of my shut down, and no results with chest fat. He told me to continue to the pills for some more time. He recommended to increase the dosage, which i questioned but for the sake of minimising my chest fat, i agreed.

He told me increasing the dosage, my sex drive will come back to normal. And i will have no performance issues. I started thinking, i came to this Guruji, with a problem of male boobs, but now he is giving me a solution to low sex drive which has been induced by his pills.

Now instead of one, i was dealing with two problems, Chest fat and low sex drive. He wanted me to be dependent on his medicines so that he could make more money by selling such pills to me. And the worse i would get, the more money he makes.

I was not too old at that time but clearly gullible. I could do anything to fix my chest fat. And such experiences i have shared in my previous bestseller book, How i fixed my chest fat in 90 days.

Things got so worse, that i literally became dependent on those medicines. These medicines were addictive and i clearly knew i had to do something to get out of this rut. I started training heavy in the gym and took control of my life ignoring my chest fat. I remember not looking at my body for one whole year. Because i knew if i would look, the ugly site of chest fat would again make me go back to that same Guruji.

And because i was young, my testosterone levels came to normal. I think they did, that is why i never felt any issues, for some time. I guess i was lucky.

Thinking about that phase, still gives me goosebumps. I was lucky i got out of it. But i still see so many men especially who are struggling with their body image, are still being victimised by such Gurujis in the name of fitness.

The reason why i am telling you this, is very simple. A quest for a great body is good. But the extreme desperation to get one, is where the danger comes in. This desperation makes us try desperate things for which we ultimately have to pay the price.

Don't just put anything into your body. If you have a problem with your sex drive or low testosterone levels, don't be desperate. Let me tell you it is normal. Acknowledge it and find a solution.

Remember, we all have a body part which we are not comfortable with. You will always two options. Option number one, to strengthen that body part or option number two, find a way to live comfortably with it. But we often choose option three, which is find a solution which gives us more problems than the one we actually had in the first place.

My problem was and sometimes it still is that i am very impatient. And often look for solutions which are quick fixes. But most often, quick fixes are temporary and give birth to a bigger problem.

Men want to be sex machines

I have a friend who is a living example of that. I know karan for many years, much before he was married. You know a friend who shares all his tiny intimate details of how many relationships he has had, who is he dating and how is his sex life etc etc. I am sure you would have friend like that. Men love boasting their sexual encounters and conquests, so they could be called Casanova, or rather popular with ladies. But when a woman does the same, she is called different names, which i don't get. But luckily things are shifting gradually.

Anyways coming back to Karan. He was one guy who would always have this constant urge to tell me about his sex life and how great he is in bed. Men get great pleasures when a woman tells him that his penis is bigger and how awesome he is in bed. We want to known as sex machine.

How many times you would come across a man who would tell you that i am a loser who don't know how to please my woman. None! You would never find a man saying that i need to learn how to give my woman a orgasm. Because men always feel they know how to please any woman. Reading and asking a woman on how i can give you more pleasure will not be good for his ego. Which actually implies, he is not great in bed and needs to work on his skills. And no man likes that.

Karan was no different. Everyday, he would come and share his stories about the girl he has been with. And how much she loves him and his ability to please her in bed. Here comes a problem.

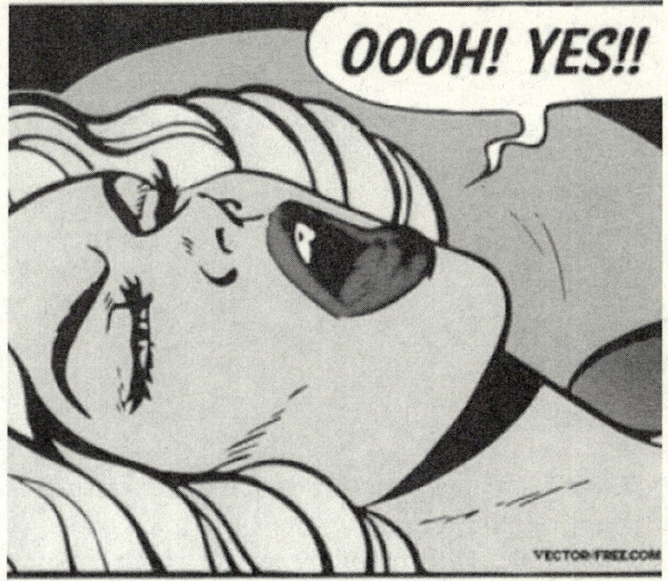


**Karan got married!**

He married his girl friend for three years and was very excited. They spent good three weeks on their honey moon and came back all refreshed. And Karan being Karan started sharing his intimate honey moon details with me. Trust me i never had to ask him to tell me such things. As i said he had this urge to share his sexual details. Don't really know if it was me or everyone. But thats besides the point.

He shared how great his honey moon was and how nothing has changed in his life after getting married. I was extremely happy to hear that. But then we had a gap of one year, Karan moved to Bangalore on a project, and got swamped with work. His work schedule got extremely hectic.

He was one guy who would have sex everyday, then it got down to once a week and eventually once a month and then once in three months. And in no time, no sex at all for a year.

I was glad he shared that with me. A guy who is apparently a sex machine and now has no time for sex. I was curious. And then what he shared was truly mind boggling.

Sex is like training. You need to do it everyday, to be in the game. This is purely a man's perspective. Apologies if i am using the word sex here instead of love making.

Karan said, because he could not find time, he was reasonably ok with that thought. Its not like its a habit, that you have to have it. After all its an emotion and for some expression of love. But the more gap he got in his sex routine, the more weary he became to have sex. And then after few weeks, sex became a routine, which he had to perform. And anything which becomes a routine, eventually gets boring. And boredom makes you want to quit.

And this exactly happened with Karan. He thought of sex as a routine, which he had to perform as a chore, since he is a husband. Because of which he lost intents in it. And this lack of interest, made him lose interest in sex. And now there he was looking for a quick fix to this problem.

Now there is no quick fix. The problem with male performance. Apologies if i give an analogy of cricket here. Every cricketer, when he is form always score back to back runs or take wickets for the team. But his lack of form starts appearing when he starts thinking of his previous bad performance!

His previous bad performance takes a toll on his current form and suddenly a player who used to score runs and take wickets doesn't even make it to the team.

Same goes for your sexual performance. If you have had performance pressure in your last sexual encounter, chances are you would still still feel the same pressure. And thinking about the previous encounter performance pressure, you would not be able to perform in the present scenario.

Sexual performance what i have realised has everything to do with your mind. Your mind needs to be in control, ignoring all the bad performances but the good scores you have had.

This was karan's problem. Because he had a terrible last sexual performance, thinking about it, made him avoid any sexual intimacy with his wife. What will she think of me that what has happened to him. Thoughts such as these ruined his mind. So he as a defense mechanism, stopped having sex completely.

And now he was looking for a quick fix. And that is why he came to me because he knew i could boost his confidence, considering he shared all his previous sexual encounters with me. Whereas he should have gone to a doctor.

I could only empathize with him and told him any friend would have said. Its all ok dude, you are the same dude, who used to have great sex few years ago. This is a phase, which shall pass too.

But what he was looking was for a quick fix, which i did not have. So he met up with our other friend, the same guy who offered me viagra. Well guess what, he offered him the same solution as well.

Fortunately he didn't have any side effect and got over his performance issues. But that was very short lived. After few weeks, he got so dependent on it, that he constantly started headaches and blurry vision. SO much so, it started affecting his daily schedule.

So he took a quick fix to make his sexual life better, but ruined his life. Till date, his vision is blurred even though sexually he is undergoing testosterone replacement therapy (TRT) which is a weekly dose of artificial testosterone injected in his body. This is a safe procedure which is performed under medical supervision. At least he got sensible but his quick fix approach gave birth to a bigger problem, his eyesight.

So there are no quick fixes. In this book i will only be sharing with you my experience which will only work if you change your lifestyle. There is no viagra pill which will make you a sex machine in hours.

In this book, i am offering a solution which has worked very well with me. This solution has come to me after speaking to hundreds of doctors and trying out many training programs, supplements and diets. What you are getting now is something which truly works. So lets go right at it.

## How i increased my testosterone levels

In this section i am sharing my experience of how you can increase your testosterone levels. More testosterone not only means more muscles but also a great sex life. I will also share a detail training plan as well, but these are the basics, which you can't ignore.

**Let go**

The one thing i have understood in life is not to take anything seriously. Because you eventually have to let go of it. So you decide how soon you want to let go. You can choose to suffer for weeks or avoid that suffering and take immediate action.

My problem was that the thought that i could not perform in bed, affected me so badly that it started to affect my life. And this thought ruined my present and made me a complete recluse. I chose no sex over having a bad experience of can't have sex. Same problem what Karan had i also developed. And i see so many men seem to be having the same problem.

Here is a solution. Talk it out with you spouse. Tell her to give you some time to recover. Keep trying with her. I know the thought of can't perform can be brutal but look at the brighter side, what if you are able to perform. That will only happen if you clear your mind.

This is my own example. I had very low testosterone levels and i could not have sex for a very long time. I was not even trying because i knew if i do, i won't be able to have sex which will further make my situation worse. But my wife was persistent, she said don't worry, i don't care, Even if you don't perform, you will still be my man. And that statement gave me so much of confidence that despite such low libido levels, i was able to have sex and that too a satisfactory one.

The point i am trying to make here is that this problem is more of a mental block, and the moment you break that block, you will be able to come out of it.

**That takes me to my next point**

**Talk to your spouse**

When you start controlling your mind, you will realise things will get much easier. and the first thing you would do then is talk to your spouse. And tell her your situation. You won't choose the route of no sex but tell her you are dealing with sexual problem which you would want to fix with her help. If she loves you, she will be more than happy to help you. Don't think like an egotistical man, but a practical man who wants a to have a great life with his wife.

This conversation will only get you much closer to your spouse. Because confronting this issue with a woman only implies that you want to make this relationship work and further strengthen the foundation of it.

Which is exactly what i did. I spoke to her and told her my situation.

And she not only understood the situation but also started looking for doctors so we could find a credible solution. Now thats what a woman would do if she loves you.

Hiding this issue, from her was anyways not working. She anyways would have found out. After all for how long you would not have sex with your partner.

**Foreplay can do wonders**

Now men as per many researches don't really enjoy the foreplay, because we want to straight to the main thing. But there is a reason why foreplay is so important. It really arouses a woman which in turn excites a man even more.

I never really paid too much attention to this sexual experience called foreplay, but after realizing its true potential, it has now become my favorite experience. When you are experiencing low libido levels, a foreplay session can really be great turn on.

Here is something i did, and yo decide weather yo chose to do it or not.

I told my wife, that because my test levels are at a all time low, please don't expect foreplay into a hardcore full blown intercourse. And as i said earlier, if a woman really wants to make things work, she will understand this problem more than you do.

**She agreed (And i thank her for that)**

And with no pressure to perform, i started enjoying the foreplay. Because i knew i could stop anywhere if i don't get a hard on. With no pressure, i somehow started loving this experience. And eventually this foreplay turned into a hardcore intercourse, without me even knowing about it.

When it comes to sex we perform better if there is no pressure to perform.

**Get your tests done**

Get your testosterone checks done every three months. And if you find it to be extremely low, like in my case, go see a doctor. Trust me there are so many solutions, that it will surprise you. And there are medications which only a doctor can prescribe after all your tests. The more you delay the visit to the doctor, the more problems you would invite to yourself.

As i said, we Indians, don't believe in going to Doctors and that too for sexual problems. I was one of those men, but now i have changed my opinion. Because i want to live a healthy sexual life.

Believe me it was a very uncomfortable the first visit but i knew if i don't, it will wreck disaster on my married life. I gradually opened up about everything. How i developed this problem, my desperation and the steroid abuse. I didn't want to hide anything because i wanted a permanent solution to this problem.

And the doctor after examining my report, gave me some herbal medicines which along with my lifestyle has worked beautifully. And i am sharing the exact same thing here with all of you.

### Avoid all drugs/steroids/medicines

All my life, i wanted to have a great physique with flat chest and great set of six pack abs.

And believe me, i have tried everything to get that dream body. It took me years to achieve a body which not only made me happy but also comfortable in my skin. But that body only looked good from the outside.

I was shallow from within by abusing so many anabolic steroids. I didn't even realise what i was doing. My focus was razor sharp to get that body i had in mind. But i didn't know i had to pay a heavy price for that.

I should have learnt from my Guruji's incident but somehow i didn't. My desperation got the better of me. This desperation made me do crazy things.

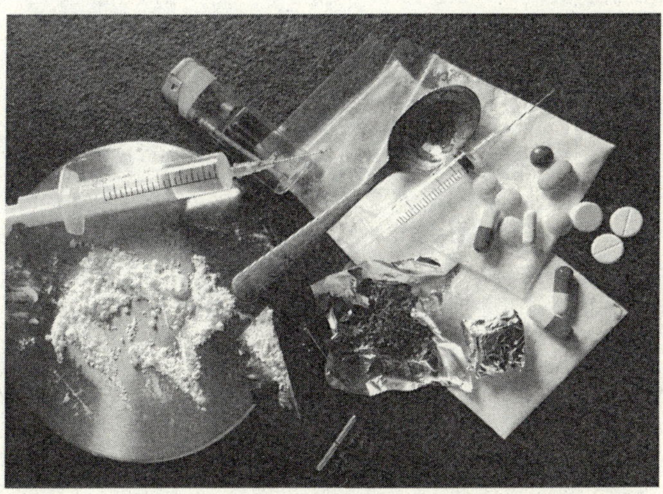

Made me try so many products, diet plans, trainingprogramsandlotsofPEDsvizperformance enhancement drugs. They eventually took a toll on my health.

No one told me how to use these anabolic steroids. All i was told was to just keep using them until you get your desired results. Which eventually lead to a complete shut down.

Our body produces testosterone naturally. It is a very smart machine. But when we start taking testosterone externally in the form of anabolic steroids, it stops producing testosterone on its own. Because the body realises that the dose is coming from the outside, no need to produce it internally. The problem comes when you stop using steroids, the body's ability to produce the same testosterone is compromised. And most of the times, it doesn't come back to normal.

**Here is an example.**

My body's testosterone level was 1000 ng/dl when i was on steroids, which is high by all standards. The normal range is around 500-600 ng/dl. But when i stopped the steroid cycle, within in days it went down to 200 ng/dl and eventually 26 ng/dl. Which lead to a complete shut down. Every man's nightmare.

| AGE | AVERAGE TESTOSTERONE LEVEL ng/dL* | 95% RANGE** |
|---|---|---|
| <25 | 692 | 376-1008 |
| 25-29 | 669 | 257-1081 |
| 30-34 | 521 | 233-1009 |
| 35-39 | 597 | 219-975 |
| 40-44 | 597 | 201-993 |
| 45-49 | 546 | 220-872 |
| 50-54 | 544 | 170-918 |
| 55-59 | 552 | 204-900 |

But there was something else also alarming in that report. My body fat had increased with elevated liver values. My liver report were of an abused alcoholic. And i have never ever touched alcohol in my life.

The doctor was concerned, and he ought to be. His exact statement was " you can't even be thinking of sex because your body has no testosterone". It was hurtful comment but i took it in my stride because it was a result of my wrong doing.

My learning is to always put your health first. It is not what looks perfect from the outside is perfect from within as well. I learnt it the hard way. You may get a great physique while you are on these drugs but you can say goodbye to your sexual performance.

It is your choice, what do you want. A great physique made by steroids or a normal healthy body with great sex life.

## Sleep quality

I never thought sleeping was this important before i actually faced this problem of low libido. My lifestyle never allowed to sleep for more than three- five hours that too in the morning wee hours. Creating content and managing three businesses was a constant struggle for me. So there were times i would sleep in the morning. Night i would use it for my content creation and working with my US team.

This disturbed my sleep pattern and literally i could never get a sound sleep. And when the doctors saw my report, they made it a point to put sound sleep on top of their prescription agenda.

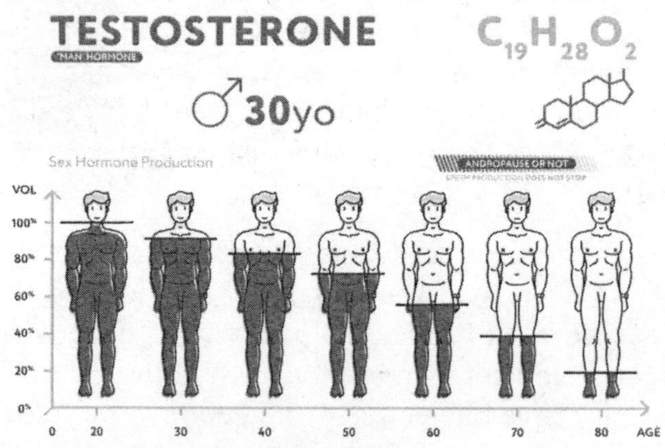

As per many researches, sleeping for less than six hours, compromises the testosterone levels by almost fifteen percent. Which means you are not allowing your body to produce enough testosterone by not sleeping enough.

I now knew i had to change this pattern. It is something i am still working on but i am now trying to sleep for more than six hours of sound sleep.

This alone is a game changer. Try sleeping for six-eight hours every night, for two weeks and see the difference. I have seen this magic work, thats why i recommend. What i have also realised that it is not just the number of hours that you sleep but the quality of sleep which actually matters. If those six hours of sleep are of sound sleep, you will see the spike in your testosterone levels for sure in few weeks. Again tired and tested.

So whatever you do, do not compromise on your sleep.

Now we have reached the main section of this book.

In this section we will discuss three main important topics which has helped me get sex drive back to normal. This is where it all boils down to!

1. Strength training
2. The diet
3. The natural supplements

## Strength training- Start lifting weights

This is where it starts! You have to start training with weights. Or i call it introducing a strength training into your regime. If you are a cardio person, or don't like the idea of going to the gym, well you have now work to do. Because now, you need to get comfortable with lifting weights.

Strength training is not only good for your health but also can do wonders for your sexual well being. But i always thought strength training can me you stiff and is only for bodybuilders or people with an aspiration to look aesthetic. I mean that is why i joined a gym because i wanted to look aesthetic.

One of the biggest myth people have about weight training is that it makes you stiff. But it is the opposite. It has some great benefits which i would like to explain.

## Minimises body fat

A good strength training session can increase your body's metabolism for 48 hours. Which means whatever you eat in that time period, your body will find a way to burn that food item. Which literally means, you will not put on extra weight or fat on your body. And lesser body fat means great muscle clarity and muscle clarity means more testosterone.

Signs Of Low Testosterone

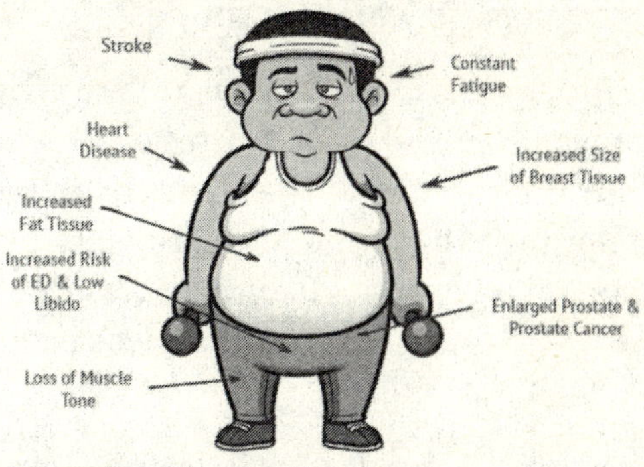


Testosterone is responsible for all the muscle growth in men. And why would you want to compromise on the muscle mass, by not training with weights! But the only catch is to acquire that muscle mass naturally not putting any synthetic hormones or steroids into it.

My goal was always to acquire the muscle mass but i lost direction and started abusing steroids. Had i stayed natural by just training with weights and manipulating the diet, i would have been in a much different position. But the only flip side to that would be that i could not have written this book.

## Improved mental health

When i lost my sex drive, i almost went into depression. So much so that i lost the appetite to eat or to even socialise with anyone. These are the crazy side effects of depression. Depression which was totally uncalled for. I know how i fought that battle. And the only thing which kept me going during this phase is weight training!

Actually the reason why i am able to write this book is because of weight training. The weight training in the gym gave me strength to face my internal demons. Also one of the biggest reasons, why my testosterone levels dipped was due to my family loss. I lost my father, who i was extremely close to.

He was one person who i shared everything with. I somehow never recovered from the loss and that trauma aggravated my anxiety and stress levels. I just completely lost the urge to have sex.

I was lucky that my wife understood my situation. But it took almost one year to get my life back to normal. And when realised i was fat with almost no sex drive left in me. When your body's test levels drop, you tend to gain unwanted fat especially from your belly and face. This exactly happened with me.

Imagine a fitness influencer with over a million social media following, who is inspiring the world to take on fitness as a lifestyle. Now is struggling to cope up with his own fitness levels. I not only gained over twelve kgs of fat but also found it extremely difficult to hit the gym.

To make things worse, i could not have sex. The thought that i have become impotent ruled my mind all the time. And the irony of that was, i had to put up fitness content everyday to keep the traction on my social media. It was a very tough time and i never thought i will be ever be able to recover from this.

But then one day, i had enough. We all need a trigger point. And that trigger always comes from within. Let me share that trigger which will blow your mind.

**The trigger point- I am not impotent**

While i was undergoing the trauma of my father's death, my wife was trying extremely hard to help me recover from it both mentally and physically. One day, she thought of giving me pleasure which every man enjoys, a blowjob.

A blowjob can turn any man into a sex maniac regardless of his test levels. But in my case even that didn't work. I could not even get a hard on with a blowjob. I not only felt embarrassed but also incapable of having and giving any sexual pleasure to my woman.

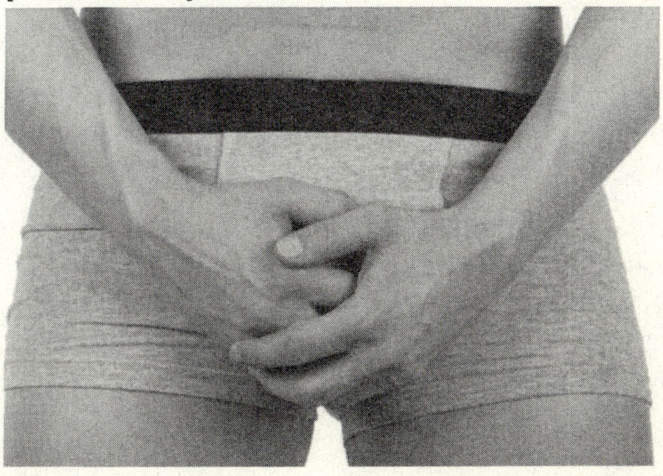

This inadequate feeling of being impotent, was good enough to take action! And that was it. i decided to change my life. I had enough of all this. I started going to the gym the very next day. I didn't think much just trained with weights.

Weights in the gym suddenly became my only friends. After few days, i started looking forward to the gym session. All i wanted was to lift. And this lifting made me do some really heavy weights. I was so broken from within, that i didn't really care if i would get injured while training. Which now in hindsight was a mistake and i would not recommend.

But this heavy lifting suddenly started helping me in my sexual life. Earlier if i didn't get the urge to do anything suddenly i started getting sexually aroused. I also started feeling the morning hardness, which was earlier missing. I could not understand what was going on. Training with weights suddenly changed gave me a new life.

Within days, i started to feel normal. My sex drive was coming back and i was feeling also very energetic and healthy. Not just that, i was looking a little more muscular than usual and my body fat was going down. I was like what is going on.

SO i started writing everything what i was doing. From training in the gym to eating every food item. After a month, i was looking at my journal, which had a training pattern and also my diet plan. I followed this plan for another four weeks and boom, it gave birth to my new program which will have a drastic effect on every man's testosterone levels. Because it worked on me, and i am the guy who possibly had the lowest test levels with zero motivation.

I further tweaked this program which i accidentally developed with so many trial and errors. I specifically added exercises which will boost test levels. I incorporated certain food items which will work great with that specific training.

This training program should only be followed for one month viz just four weeks. Because after four weeks, the result will stagnate. Even though you can continue for eight weeks, but the results would not be the same. Don't think if you follow it for the entire year, your test levels will go through the roof. No ways!

Try this program every three months for one week. But if your test levels are all time low, then you must do this for one month continuously. The program of course is unconventional and has a focus on multi-joint compound movements. Because such movement help us not only shed body fat but also increase our test levels naturally.

This is a tried and tested approach! Do not try to make any changes to this. I did this with almost every possible permutation and combination and has worked extremely well. Before this program, i didn't know that a great strength training program can drastically elevate man's test levels. Now i am a firm believer! And after this program, you will exactly know what i said what i just did.

Do not try to miss any day or deviate from the plan. Follow it for a week first and then see the results. The results will start showing in just few days.

Some things to remember- before you start following the program

You need to life your heaviest. Which means go heavy with weights. But make sure you don't get injured. Have a spotter or someone who can help you with racking and lifting.

This program works but like everybody is born different with different body types, the results may vary. If you don't see results in the first few days, don't give up, continue with the program is

You really have give your 100%. There is no shortcut to this program. If you have a medical condition or a lifestyle disease, consult your doctor before starting this program.

# THE WORK OUT

## THE TRAINING SCHEDULE

Monday

Squats 6 sets, 6 reps each

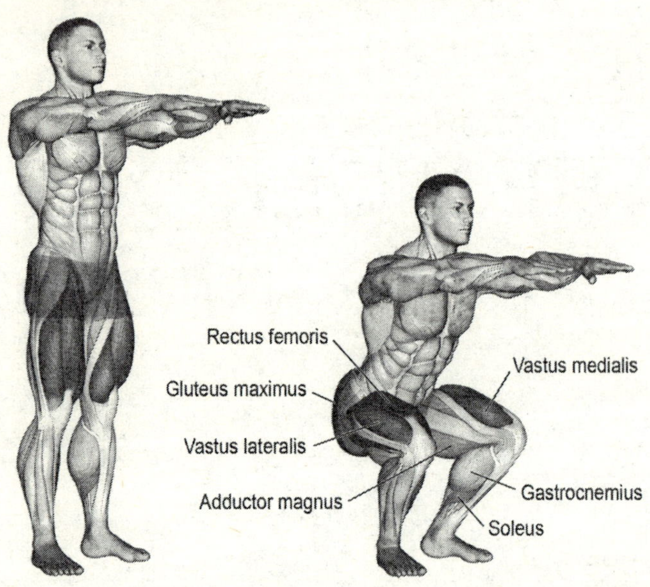

## Deadlifts, 6 sets, 6 reps each

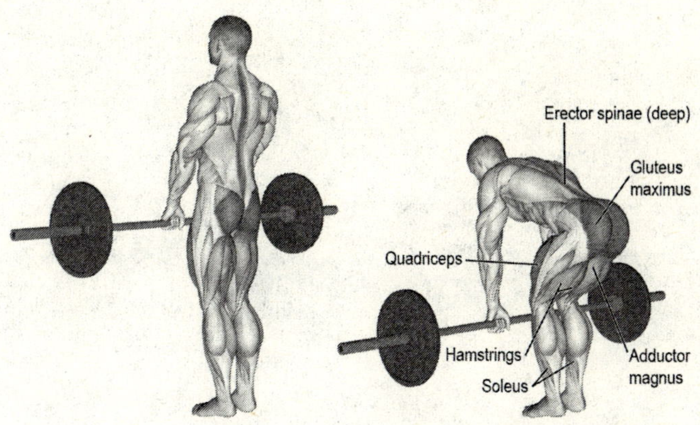


## Bench press, 6 sets, 6 reps each

Tuesday

Chest – Barbell Bench Press – 3 sets of 12 reps.

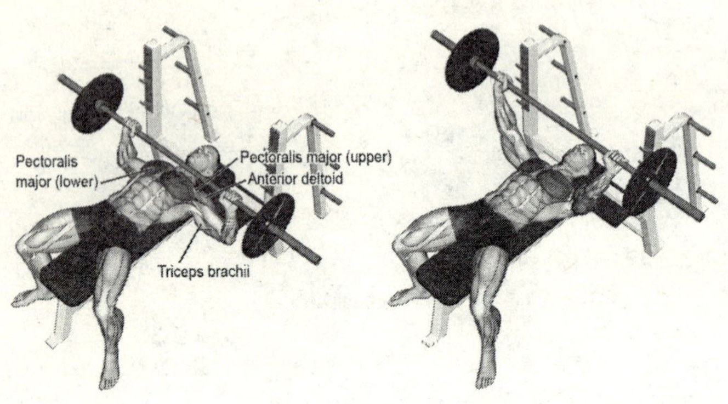


Back – Lat-pulldowns – 3 sets of 12 reps.

## Shoulders – Seated Dumbbell Press – 3 sets of 12 reps.

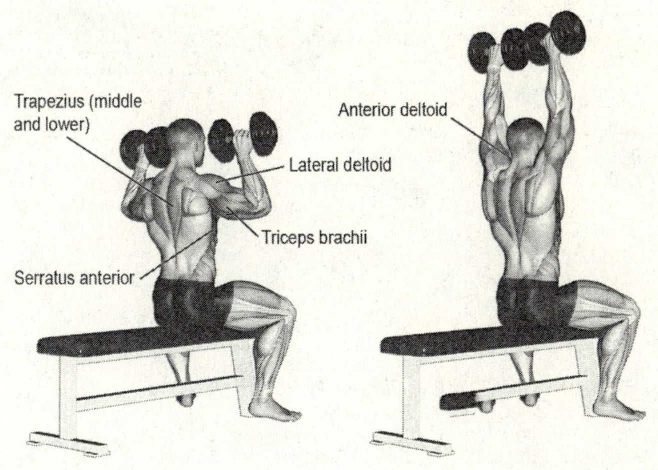


## Legs – Leg Extensions – 3 sets of 12 reps.

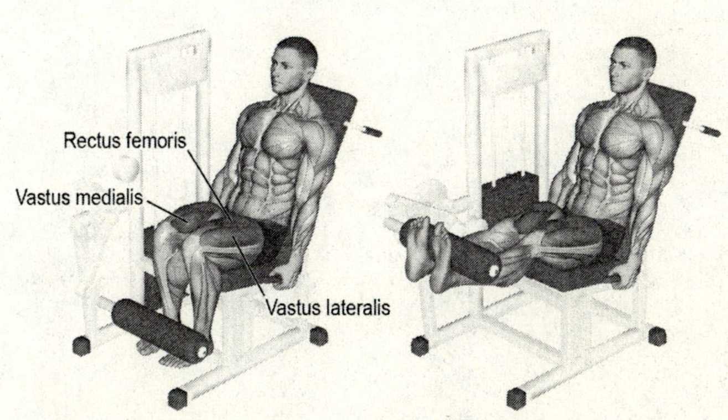

Biceps – Barbell Bicep Curls – 3 sets of 12 reps.

Triceps – Triceps Rope Pushdowns – 3 sets of 15 reps.

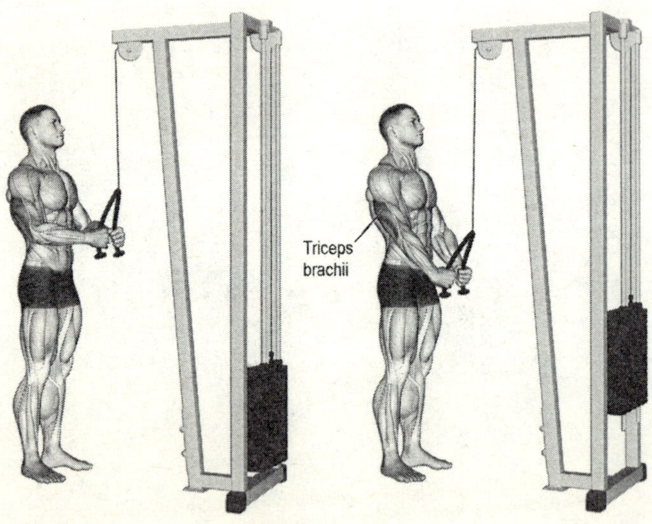

Wednesday

Legs – Leg Press Machine – 3 sets of 12 reps

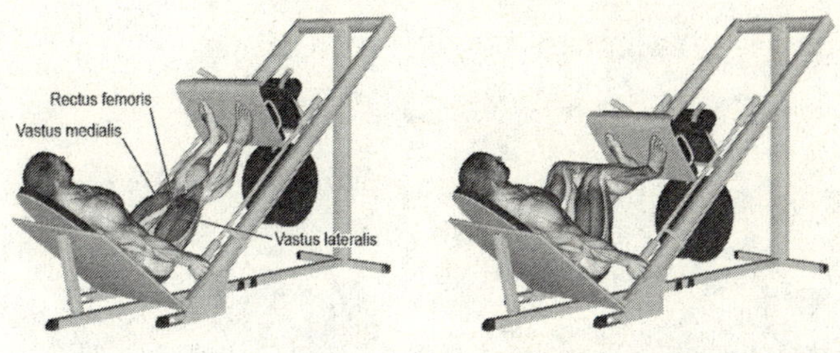


Triceps – Overhead Bar Extensions – 3 sets of 12 reps

## Biceps – EZ Bar Curls – 3 sets of 12 reps

## Chest – Machine Chest Press – 3 sets of 12 reps

## Back – T-Bar Row – 3 sets of 12 reps

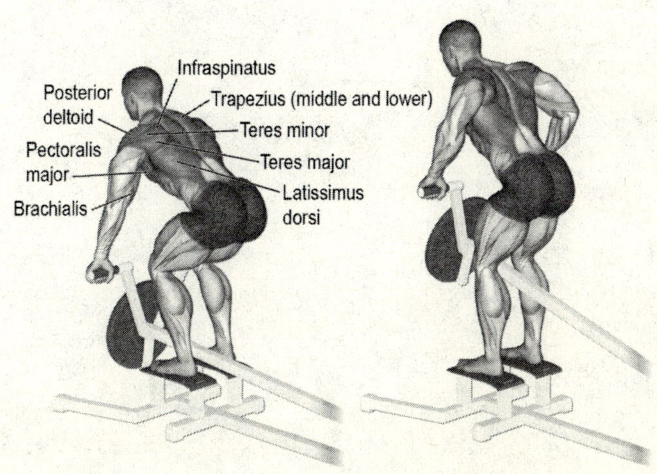

Shoulders – Lateral Raises – 3 sets of 12 reps

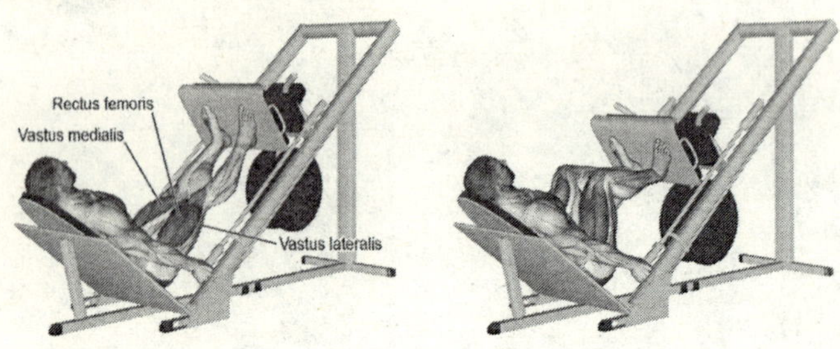


Thursday

Shoulders – EZ Bar Upright Rows – 3 sets of 12 reps

## Back – Close-Grip Pulldowns – 3 sets of 12 reps

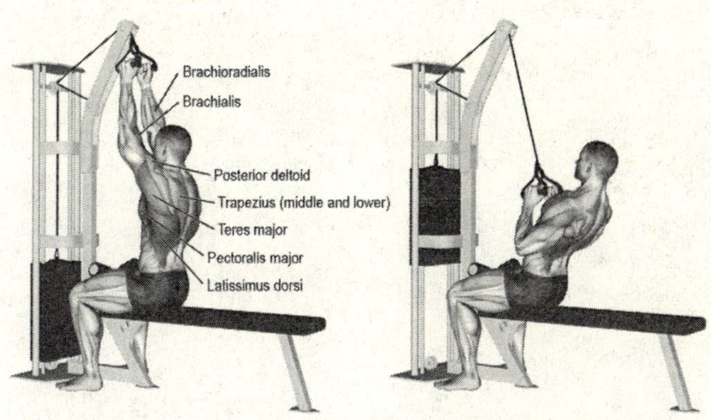


## Chest – Cable Fly – 3 sets of 12 reps

## Legs – Lunges – 3 sets of 12 reps per leg

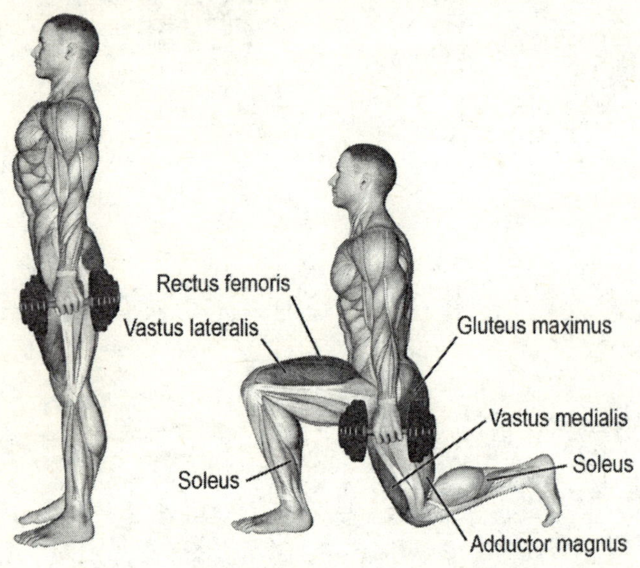

Triceps – Skullcrushers – 3 sets of 12 reps

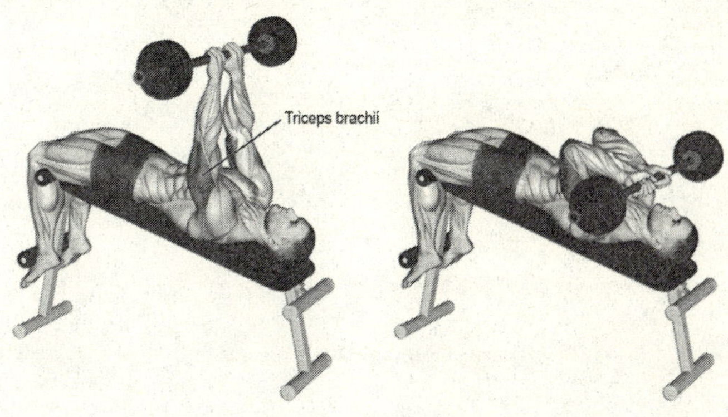


Biceps – Hammer Curls – 3 sets of 12 reps

# FRIDAY

## REST

## Saturday

## Squats 6 sets, 6 reps each

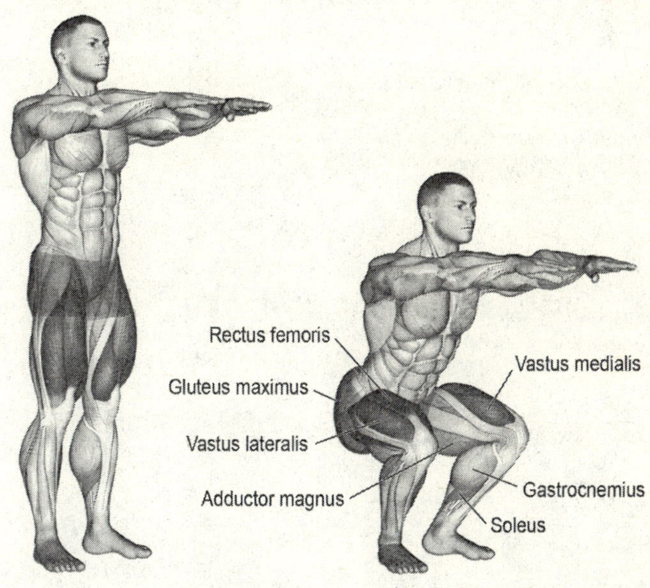


## Deadlifts, 6 sets, 6 reps each

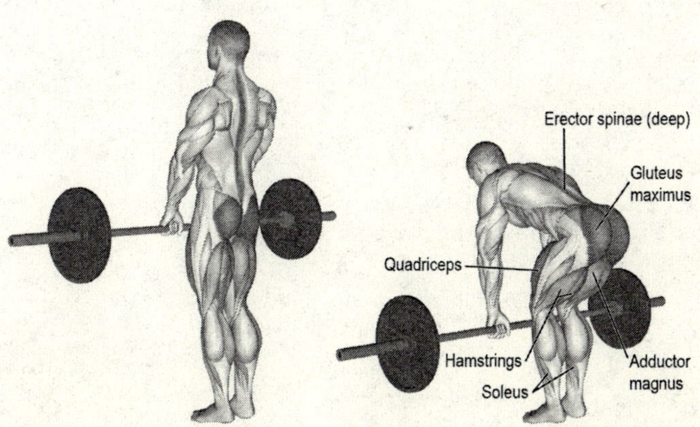

Bench press, 6 sets, 6 reps each

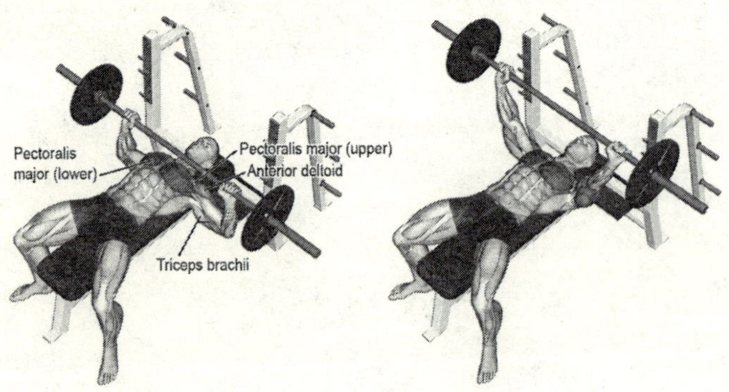

# SUNDAY

## REST

REMEMBER THIS PROGRAM IS MEANT TO SHOCK YOUR BODY AND GIVE YOU THE MUCH-NEEDED SPIKE IN YOUR TEST LEVELS.

## Fixing Low sex drive

Now before I get into the other details of what food items you should eat or what supplements you can take to fix your low sex drive, let me give you a small advise before its too late.

Having a low libido is common in today's day and age. And not fixing it on time has now become even more common. I feel lucky to address this issue on time, which is what made me write this book. Because I strongly feel, many men especially in India, will never talk about their low sex drive openly.

## When does it become a problem

As I said earlier, low sex drive either erectile dysfunction or low-test levels everything is fixable only if you treat it at the right time. There are stages, staring from mild, moderate to serious. Most of the men are caught between mild and moderate. It gets to serious because we don't consult a doctor, hoping it will cure by itself. In my opinion it doesn't get fixed on its own. It needs a treatment.

If it's mild, you can change your lifestyle, start exercising and quit alcohol and things will start looking better. But if you don't make any changes, it will get aggravated. Like it happened with my bodybuilder friend. I am only sharing this story to caution you so you take action at the earliest.

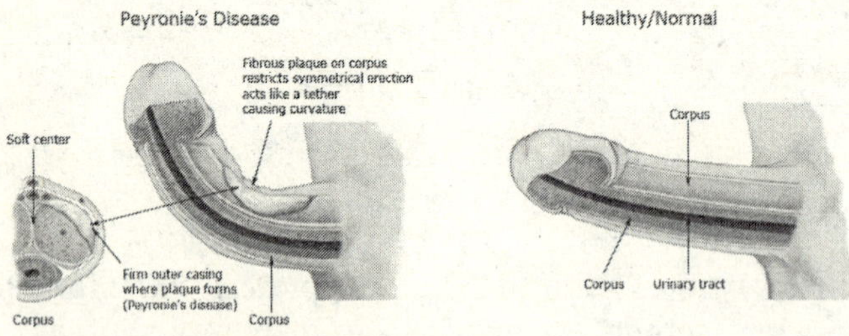


## Test levels got to zero

As India's leading fitness influencer, I get to interview people and athletes from all walks of life. This allows me to share their first hand experiences which will help each one of you struggling with this problem of low sex drive.

In my journey, I have interviewed over two hundred people including bodybuilders and most of them at some point had a problem of low libido. This is due to their strict dietary habits of no carbohydrates for days and drug use for their competition. And I came across this one athlete, who had a great physique and was winning back to back bodybuilding competitions.

He looked well conditioned and anyone who would see him would fall in love with him. He was good-looking and supremely aesthetic. Usually bodybuilders tend to cross the line between ugly and aesthetic. But he was on point with his aesthetics.

He had scheduled the interview with me, and wanted to share his fitness story with everyone. When he arrived, he was very energetic and had lots to say. And as he was sharing about his life, he reached a point, where he asked me to stop the interview. I was taken aback and didn't know what was wrong. He said, whatever I have shared in the interview is not true.

He talked about his great lifestyle and his struggle with high libido, people called me a nymphomaniac, so he said. I had no issues with anyone sharing such information so long it is useful for the audience and entertaining. But when he stopped the interview, I got worried.

And while I was thinking, on why he did that, I hear him cry. He started crying out loud. Completely oblivious to the situation, I asked him gently what seem to have happened. He after two minutes of crying told me that he is not a nymphomaniac and had made that up, just to look good. I didn't know why someone would call himself a nympho, but later I realized it was his self defense mechanism, which came off.

He could not put up with this lie on camera. Actually this is what camera does to people. It sometimes gets the worse out of you. Here I was looking at a very good looking twenty four year old with a great physique crying in front of me!

What Amrit shared is what I want I am sharing with you.

He was in his late teens when he started bodybuilding. He got a six pack to die for and a great height which made him a complete package. But when you are young, you want to try out as many things you possibly can.

He was not only using anabolic steroids for his muscle growth but also drinking alcohol every other night. The sex after alcohol was always amazing. I have even had sex with two girls in the same night. Trust me even you would believe him once you see how he looks.

I never had a steady girl friend, because I wanted to experience more and more women. I would go out almost every other night for partying with my friends, and get drunk and end up with a girl, who I barely knew (sounds like a Hollywood movie right). Everything was going right until one day, I threw up while having sex. I thought, may be I had too much to drink, so I avoided the sex and just went to bed. Recalls Amrit.

Next day I woke up, I didn't fell like doing anything. I was feeling terrible and extremely weak. I chose to rest that day even skipped my gym session. I thought this was normal so after a day's rest I started my gym and the partying lifestyle. To my surprise, i could not have sex because I kept feeling pukish and my inability to not perform the last time.

What was happening to me! As a twenty year old you would think, the problem will subside in days. But it only got worse. So much so that I started avoiding sex. This avoidance made me indulge into alcohol even more. And within three months, I became alcoholic, no could not have sex.

It didn't stop just there! I was also competing in bodybuilding competitions. Which made me do crazy diet routines with excessive amount of steroid use to win competitions. Even though I was winning competitions but the fact that I could not have sex, was killing me from within.

I should have spoken to a doctor but I was too embarrassed to! And within days, the problem got so worse, that even my body started giving up on me. I became very unhappy, and become a drug addict as well. Tried cocaine in desperation only so I could have sex. But of no luck!

My problem had now become more of a mental block that a physical one. Even though I would get high and aroused, I could not have sex thinking I cant have sex only. I should have seeked help but it became so bad that now I have completely screwed up my hormones.

Finally I reached a stage of suicide where I had no other option but to go to a doctor. And the doctor got my testosterone levels checked and the results were shocking. My test numbers were in minus. My body was not producing any testosterone naturally. I had a complete shut down. And this happened due to my drinking habits primarily.

You can be young and still face issues with low libido, if your lifestyle is of drinking.

Doctors have now stopped my alcohol consumption and even steroid usage. Its been almost six months, that I am trying to recover. Not too sure if it is working or not. But I broke down when I had to tell a lie about being a nympho. I am even struggling to get a hard on. This was the reason why I was crying. Added Amrit.

Obviously I edited his sex life part from the interview, but there was great learning from Amrit. The day he puked, he should have gone to the doctor the next day. He kept avoiding and eventually compromised on his health. He should have added some food items, which would have helped him but he chose not to.

Now for you to avoid that situation, I am sharing the food items you can have ot increase your sex drive. They helped me a lot. I never thought adding small food items can work so well with my libido. But the training program backed by this food item, is a sure shot game changer.

Food items to increase the sex drive

## Walnuts

I was never a dry fruit fan especially walnuts (akhrot). I was a non believer questioning food items and their potency to increase sex drive. But when you have nothing to lose and everything to gain, you don't really mind trying out things you never have before. Walnuts are one of them!

Walnuts have great benefits. Not only they improve the quality of sperm but also improve the shape, movement and vitality of the sperm. Besides increase the libido it also improves the fertility of the sperm.

There is no best time to have them, you can have them anytime you want! Besides it has many other health benefits. Walnuts are rich in omega-3 fats and contain higher amounts of antioxidants than most other foods. Eating walnuts may improve brain health and prevent heart disease and cancer.

## Strawberries

The seeds of these strawberries are loaded with zinc which is essential for sex for both, men and women. Don't you always see in movies especially Hollywood, Champaign and strawberries before making out. Now you know why!

The best time to have strawberries is before your sex. Think of it as your pre sex fruit. I didn't know the power of it, until I tried it. I didn't feel much the first time I had it but the second time, I could totally feel the difference. There is a good reason for it.

Strawberries are loaded with zinc and zinc levels reduce during intercourse. So for a longer session, strawberries can play a key role. Plus there are many other benefits of strawberries. One major benefit I found it useful was that strawberries could get you in good mood.

The seeds of strawberries contain the omega-3 fatty acid alpha-linolenic acid, which has been proven to improve mood. Now if you had a long day at work or have high stress levels, having some strawberries can help. Now again this would only work if you make an effort. If you would expect strawberries to do all the trick that wont happen. You need to first relax and calm down for strawberries to work. Remember it's a fruit not an anti depressant or Viagra.

## Watermelon

Without getting any technical, let me explain why watermelon is good for increasing our libido. Watermelon contains an amino acid called citrulline, which helps the blood help to our sexual organs. A steady blood flow means harder and longer erection. Technically, it works exactly like Viagra, but minus the side effects of Viagra.

I never liked watermelon as a fruit earlier, but after knowing the sexual benefits of it, I began experimenting. And man! I was amazed to see the results. The best time to have a watermelon is in the afternoon.

Plus the other benefit I feel is worth mentioning is its ability to help us recover from muscle soreness. Now as a routine, after my work out routine, I ensure I have some watermelon during the day.

## Almonds

Not sure if you would know, but Almonds contain arginine, which also improves circulation of blood vessels. Arginine found in almonds helps us maintain an erection.

Now go back a few years and ask yourself why people back in the old days always had soaked almonds on bedside for the newly wed groom for his first night. Almonds are great for your sexual health.

No wonder since ancient times, body builders, wrestlers, and professional fighters incorporated almonds in their daily diet as their main staple. Even today if you travel in small Indian cities, the wrestlers main source of energy are almonds. Not only they are good for our strength, but also help us maintain the sexual strength.

If you are struggling with premature ejaculation, almonds can be your best bet. I incorporated them with my breakfast, that too 10 of them. Soak them overnight and have them in the morning with your breakfast and then see the magic. Not only it will help you lift better in the gym but also help you perform better in bed.

## Chocolate

Now don't go gorge on chocolates thinking its good for sex. First its dark chocolate and second there is a way to have chocolate. Just like strawberries, consume chocolate as a pre snack before your intercourse.

I made a mistake of consuming chocolates after every meal thinking it will help me with my sex. But it only got me fatter, which is obviously not what you want.

Remember, chocolate gets into a good mood. Phenylethylamine, a neuronal released by the brain, is also found in chocolate, and induces a sense of euphoria during the intercourse, by turning on the brain's pleasure nuclei. This molecule increases the feeling of excitement and boosts the sex drive; consequently, it gives you more or less the same sensation that the alcohol does, but without the secondary effects of the latter.

Now you know why it is important to know the timing of consuming a chocolate- **ALWAYS BEFORE THE INTERCOURSE.**

## Eggs

In my discovery, I found out that there are certain food items, which are supposed to be taken before the intercourse and some as part of the daily diet. Eggs are one such item, which should be added as a daily go to food.

Not only they are rich in proteins, but also great for healthy erection. Eggs contain amino acid L-arginine that can improve erectile dysfunction.

Besides, eggs are a must have if you are trying to pack on muscles. They are considered to be one of the most effective protein sources available in the market.

Eggs are rich in vitamins B6 and B5. These help balance hormone levels and fight stress, two things that are crucial to a healthy libido.

Now I have also tried on someone's recommendation to have eggs before the intercourse! Again I didn't have a good experience, not because it had a foul smell, I mean that too, but it did not work for me. Some people seem to have great results eating raw chicken eggs just prior to sex is said to heighten libido and maximize energy levels. **AGAIN, YOU CAN TRY, WHO KNOWS IT MAY WORK**

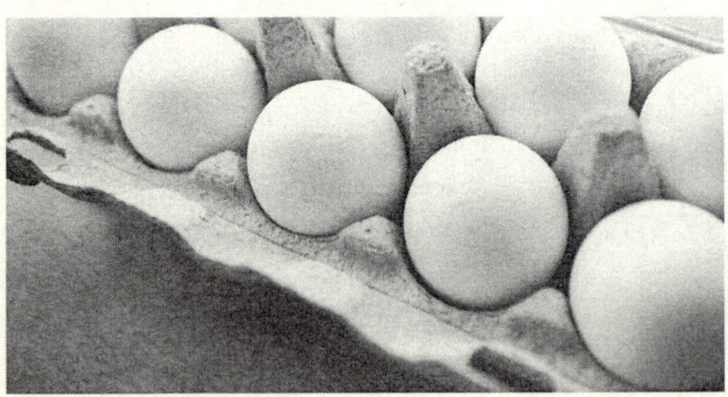

## Garlic

Now I certainly don't recommend having garlic before the intercourse, because that would be last intercourse of your life with the same partner. You still want to know why? Ofcourse the smell! Have mercy on the partner please.

Then how else you would want reap the benefits of garlic for sexual pleasure.

Garlic contains allicin, an ingredient that increases blood flow to the sexual organs. Exactly what you need for a good healthy erection. But the problem is the smell, so instead go for some garlic pills! Yes they are available in the market. The smell of garlic can be a mood killer but the benefits will force you to have some pills.

If not, you can always find out ways to add garlic into your diet, because it also has some great medicinal properties. Garlic is known to help us combat common cold. But you don't really care about such properties right now, so stick to the pills instead and see how that works for you.

## Coffee

Opinion on the benefits of coffee is divided across the world. But most of them believe that coffee is one stimulant, which can be great before sex. Because it is a stimulant, it can really heighten the arousal.

Scientists believe it could be because the caffeine triggers a chemical reaction that increases blood flow to the penis by relaxing muscles. But scientists believe in many things, which I didn't believe in. So I tried this one! And guess what, even I also now believe in these scientists.

I remember having a black coffee before my work out session. And those work outs were always great. So one day after reading about it, I thought why not reap the same benefit in my sexual work out. If you were to analyse it, sex is also somewhat like a work out. But the working muscles in sex is different which needs constant blood flow to maintain erection.

That is why we by having food items before sex, we are ensuring we don't fall short of that blood supply. Coffee is a stimulant which ensures, we have energy in abundance, which is exactly what is required if you need to satisfy your partner.

Now let me share some techniques which are old school in nature but have come very handy to me in getting my sex drive back

Believe it or not, this will have a positive effect on your libido.

## Kegel exercises – GAME CHANGER

Kegels are exercises that help you strengthen muscles below the bladder that help control urination. Kegel exercises can strengthen the pelvic floor muscles –the group of muscles, which help increase blood flow to the groin and are active during sex. Did you know strengthening the pelvic floor muscles can improve sexual function, such as erections, orgasms and ejaculations.

The problem with most of the men in India is that they don't even know what kegel is! Did you know what kegel exercises are! Did you know the benefits of kegel exercises. This is exactly what I did for one month and was amazed to see the results.

Arnold Kegel first described the exercises in 1948, and historically the exercises treated female patients following childbirth health issues. But with time pelvic floor muscle therapy have been demonstrated to be useful in a variety of conditions, including erectile dysfunction and premature ejaculation. Unlike typical exercise routines, these exercises don't require the participant to buy any weights or expensive machines. However, the success of Kegel exercises is dependent on proper performance of the exercises. You just have to do it right for it to work, period.

## Doing Kegel exercises

First find the right muscles

To identify your pelvic floor muscles, stop urination in midstream or tighten the muscles that keep you from passing gas. These maneuvers use your pelvic floor muscles. Once you've identified your pelvic floor muscles, you can do the exercises in any position, although you might find it easiest to do them lying down at first.

Second practice your technique

Tighten your pelvic floor muscles, hold the contraction for three seconds, and then relax for three seconds. Try it a few times in a row. When your muscles get stronger, try doing Kegel exercises while sitting, standing or walking.

Third, maintain your focus

For best results, focus on tightening only your pelvic floor muscles. Be careful not to flex the muscles in your abdomen, thighs or buttocks. Avoid holding your breath. Instead, breathe freely during the exercises.

Repeat 3 times a day. Do at least three sets of 10 repetitions a day.

## When to do your Kegels

Make Kegel exercises part of your daily routine. For example: Fit in a set of Kegel exercises every time you do a routine task, such urinating- Do a set after you urinate, to get rid of the last few drops of urine. DON'T GO BY THE SOUND OF IT, IT IS TRIED AND TESTED BY MANY PEOPLE ACROSS THE WORLD

## How to perform kegel

Stop urination mid-flow

While you are urinating, attempt to stop and start your urine stream. The muscles you use to do this are your pelvic floor muscles. These are the muscles you are trying to target.

Don't make it a practice. This method should only be used to find your pelvic floor muscles.

## Squeeze your anus muscles

Contract the anus muscles you normally use to prevent yourself from passing gas, or to hold in a bowel movement. If you perform a squat movement, this should not be difficult for you at all. Even it is difficult, you now need to master it.

You know you are performing the exercise correctly when you feel a lifting or pulling sensation on your anus

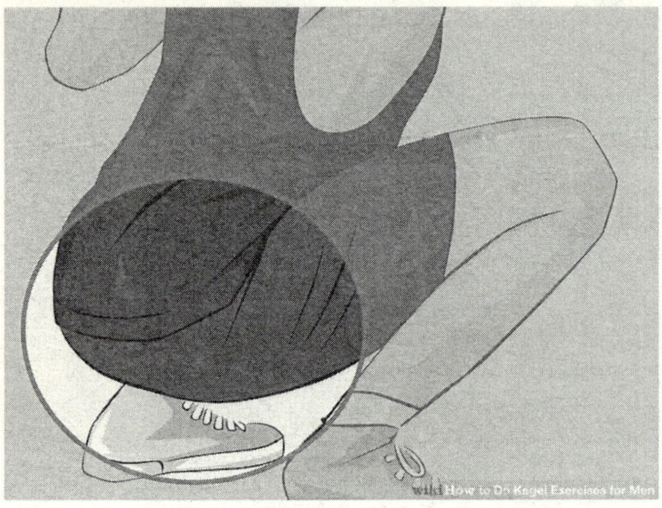


Stand in front of the mirror.

Well this could be funny for some but try to lift your penis vertically while keeping your buttocks, abdominal and thigh muscles still. And you have to perform this while looking yourself in the mirror. If you notice yourself tightening your buttocks, thigh or abdominal muscles, then stop the exercise and try again.

## Practicing Kegel

Do the exercises while lying down. Lie down on a mat or your bed. Contract and hold your pelvic floor muscles for five seconds. Do this without contracting your buttocks, abdomen or thigh muscles. Then relax them for five seconds and repeat the exercise.

Because it is easier to do Kegel exercises while lying down, start out by doing them this way first if you are a beginner.

When you first start doing the exercises, start out slowly by doing only five reps at a time. Do a set of five reps twice a day; for example, in the morning and at night. Do this every day

Once you have perfected the first movment then move on to this squat position.

On your second week, do a set of ten reps three times per day. You can do them in the morning, during your lunch break, and before you go to bed. Do this five to seven times per week.

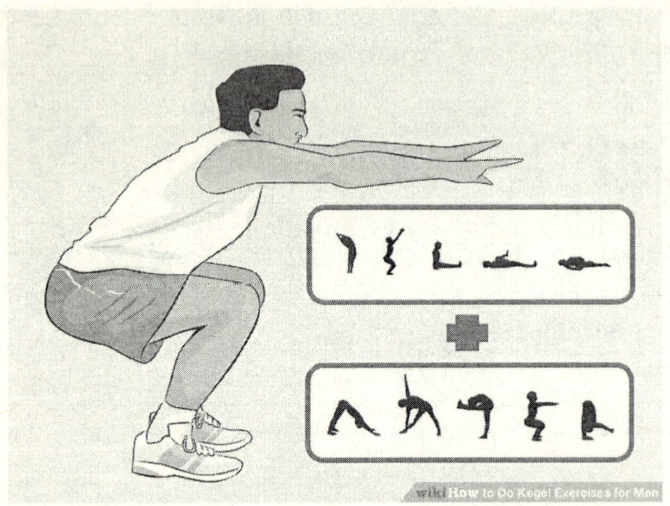

## The supplements

The training and diet mentioned in this book is good enough to spike up your libido and testosterone levels. But i have also used certain natural supplements to help me combat the problem of low sex drive.

These supplements have almost zero side effects. But again this has been my experience. And I would strongly recommend speak to your general physician before taking any of these supplements. Even I consulted many doctors before I used these natural supplements. Because sometimes these so called supplements can have a reverse effect. Which means consuming such supplements can further aggravate the problem of low testosterone levels.

This is because everybody is different with a different body type. Our bodies react differently to different medicines and food items. What may work on me may not necessarily work on you. Therefore I would recommend speaking to your doctor before consuming any of this.

## Ashwagandha

Ashwagandha is one of the most ancient herbs in Ayurveda, a form of alternative medicine based on Indian principles of natural healing. I found ashwagandha an extremely potent solution in fixing low sex drive.

To my surprise it was also helping me with increased energy levels in the gym. When I researched I found it that it has been used for over 3,000 years to relieve stress, increase energy levels and improve concentration

"Ashwagandha" is Sanskrit for "smell of the horse," which refers to both its unique smell and ability to increase strength. I bet you didn't know that.

Plus it is readily available across India at a very cost effective price point. It is certainly not an expensive solution. But the only downside of it is that it works very slowly. If you think it works instantly like Viagra, you would be extremely disappointed. It takes weeks for it to work, that too with a training program, which I have mentioned earlier in this book.

## Tribulus

Tribulus terrestris has been my go to supplement and is one of my favorites. It is a herb that has been used for centuries in herbal medicine with great results. It is a small leafy plant called Gokshura in India.

Again this is a natural remedy, which is being used for years. My experience with tribulus has been great. I have been taking it for almost one year. This is one of the natural testosterone boosters, which every man should use. Because this works.

One 90-day study in men with erectile dysfunction found that taking tribulus improved self-reported ratings of sexual health and increased testosterone levels by 16%.

But again, as I said, it may work wonders for some and some may not feel any changes supplementing with it.

## Zinc

Did you know, zinc is an essential mineral involved in more than 150 chemical processes within the body! Our zinc levels within the body have been closely associated with testosterone levels

In our program, you will get greatly benefited from zinc. Because it is helpful in recovering from brutal work outs.

The researchers found significant benefits for those with low levels, including increased testosterone and sperm count.

In elite wrestlers, taking zinc each day also helped reduce a decline in testosterone levels following a 4-week high-intensity training regimen